# ENROUTE-Rx:
# AT THE CROSSROADS OF ETERNITY

*A Biblical Exploration of Death, Grief, and Eternal Hope*

Shawn E. Wells, LFD, BCCC, CGC

This book is intended for educational and spiritual encouragement purposes only. It is not intended to replace medical, psychiatric, psychological, or professional counseling services. Readers experiencing severe depression, thoughts of self-harm, or emotional crisis are strongly encouraged to seek immediate assistance from qualified healthcare professionals or emergency services.

ISBN: 979-8-9946309-3-8

Printed in the United States of America

First Edition

# DEDICATION

To every believer who has stood in the quiet after the funeral. To those who have loved deeply and therefore grieved deeply. To families who carried faith through hospital rooms, hospice halls, and silent homes.

And to those who are walking forward with tears in their eyes and eternity in their hearts.

May this book steady your steps at life's final crossroads.

# SCRIPTURE NOTICE

This book is written with the assumption that the reader is a believer in Jesus Christ. It does not seek to introduce faith for the first time, but to remind the faithful of what they already know and sometimes struggle to feel during grief.

Scripture is foundational throughout these pages. The Bible is not presented as theory, but as truth. It is the anchor for understanding death, suffering, endurance, and hope.

The Holy Bible has often been described as "Basic Information Before Leaving Earth." In the context of grief, it becomes more than information. It becomes direction. It becomes assurance. It becomes steady ground at the crossroads of eternity.

All Scripture quotations are taken from the King James Version (KJV) and the New International Version (NIV), as noted.

May the Word of God speak clearly, comfort deeply, and anchor firmly as you walk this journey by faith.

# PREFACE

This book along with Funeral Service at a Crossroads and ENROUTE-Rx, was always meant to stand together.

Funeral Service at a Crossroads was written for the profession. It challenged funeral directors and leaders to examine our calling, ethics, and responsibility in serving families during life's most sacred moments.

ENROUTE-Rx was written for families navigating the days before and beyond the funeral.

But something deeper remained.

In both works, I recognized that grief is not only emotional and not only practical. At its core, grief is spiritual. It forces us to confront eternity. It exposes what we believe about God, about suffering, about death, and about what lies beyond it.

This book lives in that space.

ENROUTE-Rx: At the Crossroads of Eternity does not merely discuss death. It confronts the spiritual foundation of who we are. It addresses the reality that every human being will one day stand at the crossroads of eternity — either beside someone we love, or personally at the threshold.

The Bible has often been described as "Basic Information Before Leaving Earth." In seasons of grief, that description becomes more than clever than phrasing. It becomes an essential truth. Scripture does not avoid sorrow. It does not deny suffering. It does not silence questions. Instead, it provides clarity, direction, and eternal perspective.

This book assumes faith. It is written not to persuade unbelief, but to steady the believe. It is a reminder that grief does not erase the Gospel. It tests it. It deepens it. It refines it.

You will find here an honest examination of the stages of grief. You will encounter discussions of anger, guilt, depression, and surrender. You will see mental health addressed responsibly. You will be reminded to care for your body as well as your soul. You will be challenged not to idolize sorrow or accuse God, but to anchor yourself in eternity.

If Funeral Service at a Crossroads called the profession to reflection, and ENROUTE-Rx walked beside families in grief, this book calls the believer to spiritual alignment at life's most serious intersection.

Death is certain. Eternity is real. Christ is risen.

That is the foundation upon which every page rests.

Shawn E. Wells, LFD, BCCC, CGC

# INTRODUCTION

The graveside wind was stronger than expected. The family stood in a tight semicircle; coats pulled close; eyes fixed on the casket as it rested above the earth. The prayer had been spoken. The final hymn had faded. But no one moved. A grown son stared downward as if waiting for someone to explain what came next. A widow's hand trembled in mine. In that silence, theology was no longer abstract. Resurrection was no longer a doctrine discussed in church. It was the only thing standing between despair and endurance.

Death Does Not Come With Instructions

Death does not come with instructions.

It does not arrive with a manual explaining how to feel, what to say, or how long sorrow should last. It does not pause us emotionally. Even when we know it is coming, we are rarely ready for the weight of it.

As believers, we understand eternity. We believe in heaven. We believe in resurrection. We believe that death has been defeated through Christ. And yet when loss enters our lives, our theology is tested in ways we did not anticipate.

Faith does not eliminate grief. It confronts it.

Grief exposes what we believe. It reveals whether our understanding of eternity is theoretical or anchored. It uncovers assumptions we did not know we held. It forces us to wrestle not only with absence, but with identity, sovereignty, and trust.

This book is not written to remove sorrow. It is written to align sorrow with Scripture. It is not written to silent emotions. It is written to steady it. It assumes you believe. It assumes you trust Christ. But it also assumes you are human — and that grief can shake even steady faith.

For years, I have stood beside families in hospital rooms, funeral homes, and gravesides. I have watched strong believers tremble. I have listened to whispered questions after the service ends and the crowd disperses. I have seen how grief lingers long after the final prayer is spoken. As a licensed funeral director and Christian counselor, I have learned that the most difficult conversations often happen in private, when theology meets reality. This book was shaped in those moments.

Death confronts every person eventually. It confronts us when we lose someone we love. It confronts us when we consider our own mortality. It confronts us in hospital rooms, at gravesides, and in quiet homes long after the funeral has ended.

What death does not provide; Scripture does.

The Bible does not offer step-by-step emotional instructions, but it does provide eternal direction. It reminds us that sorrow is real, but not ultimate. It teaches that tears are permitted, but despair is not sovereign. It anchors us in the truth that separation in Christ is temporary.

In the pages ahead, we will examine the stages of grief honestly. We will confront anger without sin. We will address false guilt. We will discuss depression responsibly. We will speak about medication without shame and psychoeducation without fear. We will guard against idolizing grief and against accusing God. We will examine what it means to walk forward without being betrayal.

Above all, we will keep eternity in view.

This book is not about escaping grief. It is about enduring it with clarity. It is not about feeling stronger. It is about standing anchored. It is not about having every answer. It is about trusting the One who does.

Death does not come with instructions.

But it does reveal what is true.

It reveals whether Christ is truly our hope.
It reveals whether eternity is truly our anchor.
It reveals whether resurrection is truly our confidence.

At life's final crossroads, belief must become a conviction. Conviction must become endurance. Endurance must become a steady faith.

Christ is risen.
Heaven is certain.
Death is not the end.

Stand there.
Stand anchored.
Stand in hope.

Everything else flows from that foundation.

# TABLE OF CONTENTS

# CHAPTER 1

## Anticipatory Grief: Preparing Before the Loss

There is a grief that begins before death ever occurs. It does not wait for the final breath. It does not require a funeral. It begins quietly in hospital rooms, in long-term diagnoses, in aging parents who move more slowly than before, in conversations that carry an unspoken weight. This is anticipatory grief. It is the sorrow of knowing that loss is coming.

Many believers feel confused or even ashamed during this stage. They ask themselves why they feel sadness when their loved one is still alive. They wonder if grieving early means a lack of faith. It does not. Anticipatory grief is not unbelief. It is love recognizing the possibility of separation.

When you love deeply, you sense vulnerability. When someone's health declines or time appears limited, your heart begins adjusting before your mind is ready. You may notice waves of sadness while sitting beside them. You may feel moments of panic when imagining life without their presence. You may rehearse conversations in your mind that have not yet happened. None of this makes you disloyal. It makes you human.

Scripture does not condemn preparation. In fact, wisdom encourages it. Jesus prepared His disciples for His departure. He spoke openly about what was coming. He did not hide reality from them. He told them not to let their hearts be troubled, but He did not deny that trouble would come. Faith does not ignore what is approaching. It faces it anchored in truth.

Anticipatory grief often carries mixed emotions. You may feel sadness and gratitude at the same time. You may feel closeness and fear together. You may feel relief if suffering appears near its end, and then feel guilty for that relief. This emotional complexity is normal. Grief is rarely simple.

During this stage, the mind attempts to protect itself. You may begin imagining what you will say at the funeral. You may think about practical arrangements. You may worry about unresolved conflict. These thoughts are not morbid. They are signs that your heart is trying to prepare.

Preparation, however, must remain balanced. There is danger in pretending death is not coming, and there is danger in obsessing over it constantly. Wisdom lives between denial and fixation. You can acknowledge reality without surrendering to fear.

This stage offers opportunities. Conversations that might have been postponed can be spoken now. Words of forgiveness can be exchanged. Gratitude can be expressed clearly. Spiritual assurance can be reaffirmed. If the person you love is able, pray together. Read Scripture together. Speak honestly about eternity. These moments become sacred.

You may also feel anxiety during this season. The unknown can be unsettling. Questions about timing, medical decisions, and about the future may circulate repeatedly. Bring those concerns to God daily. Do not wait until death occurs to begin leaning into His presence. Preparation is not a lack of faith. It is a strengthening of it.

False guilt often tries to enter here as well. You may feel that grieving early means you are giving up. It does not. You are not surrendering hope. You are acknowledging vulnerability. You can pray for healing while still preparing your heart for loss. Faith and preparation are not enemies.

Physically, anticipatory grief can produce fatigue and tension. You may find it difficult to focus at work. You may feel emotionally drained even before death occurs. Care for your body now. Eat properly. Rest intentionally. Speak with someone safe about what you are experiencing. Serious seasons require serious listeners. Not everyone is equipped to carry these conversations, but someone is.

Anticipatory grief also sharpens perspective. It reminds you that life is temporary. It clarifies priorities. Small arguments feel less important. Presence becomes more valuable than productivity. Eternity feels closer.

This stage is not about controlling the outcome. It is about stewarding the time that remains. You cannot determine the day or the hour. You can determine how you love it. You can choose honesty over avoidance. You can choose gratitude over silence. You can choose spiritual grounding over panic.

If healing comes, you will be grateful. If death comes, you will know you did not waste the opportunity to prepare. Either way, you walk forward anchored in Christ.

Anticipatory grief is not premature sorrow. It is protective love adjusting to possibility. It allows the heart to begin bending before it is forced to break. When the moment finally arrives, you will not be untouched by pain, but you will not be unprepared in faith.

Stand steady in this season. Speak about what matters. Pray without ceasing. Love intentionally. Eternity is not a distant concept. It is a present reality shaping how you live today.

# CHAPTER 2

## At the Crossroads: When Death Becomes Reality

There will be moments when prayer feels thin, and words feel insufficient. This is where worship can carry you. Sometimes a song articulates what your heart cannot. The testimony of survival sung by voices like Marvin Sapp reminds us that endurance itself becomes evidence of grace. The honesty often heard in Kirk Franklin's music reflects imperfect faith persevering through real pain. Worship in grief does not deny sorrow. It declares that sorrow does not have final authority. Let worship minister when your voice is weak and your strength feels distant.

When death occurs, the body reacts before theology does. You may experience numbness, confusion, strange calm, sudden tears, or overwhelming exhaustion. This is not a spiritual weakness. It is a neurological shock. God designed the human body with protective mechanisms. When something overwhelming occurs, the brain softens the emotional impact temporarily. This is mercy, not malfunctioning. Even faithful believers experience shock. In John 11, when Lazarus died, Jesus wept. He knew resurrection was coming. He knew death was not permanent. Yet He still wept. "Jesus wept" (John 11:35 KJV; NIV). Two words. Eternal weights. Grief does not contradict faith; it confirms love.

At this crossroads, three temptations often arise. The first is to collapse into despair. The second is to harden into emotional shutdown. The third is to spiritualize pain prematurely. Some believers rush to statements meant to comfort — "They're in a better place," or "It was God's will" — but when spoken too quickly, such phrases can silence necessary lament. Faith does not erase grief. It gives grief direction. We are not called to suppress sorrow; we are called to anchor it.

There is a difference between lament and accusation. David was lamented. Job questioned. Christ cried out from the cross. Yet none placed God on trial. You may say, "Lord, this hurts," or "I do not understand." You may bring confusion and sorrow honestly before Him. But guard against accusing God of injustice. The cross reminds us that God is not distant from suffering; He entered it. Isaiah describes Christ as "a man of sorrows and acquainted with grief" (Isaiah 53:3 KJV), "a man of suffering, and familiar with pain" (NIV). We do not worship a detached God. We worship One who understands burial.

In the first days after death, spiritual focus must also include physical stewardship. Grief places stress on the body. My appetite may fade. Sleep may be disrupted. Cortisol rises, and blood pressure can fluctuate. This is not a lack of faith; it is biology. Scripture reminds us that our bodies are temples of the Holy Spirit (1 Corinthians 6:19 KJV; NIV). Caring for your body in grief is not indulgent — it is obedient. Eat something simple. Drink water. Rest when you can. Move gently. These small acts stabilize the storm.

There will be moments when prayer feels thin, and words feel insufficient. This is where worship can carry you. Sometimes a song articulates what your heart cannot. The testimony of survival sung by artists like Marvin Sapp reminds us that endurance itself becomes evidence of grace. The declarations of freedom voiced by Tasha Cobbs echo the truth that grief may bind temporarily, but it does not own the believer. The honesty often heard in Kirk Franklin's music reflects imperfect faith persevering through real pain. Let worship minister when your voice is weak.

At the crossroads of eternity, return to what you know. Death is an enemy, but it is a defeated one. Resurrection is not a metaphor; it is a promise. Separation in Christ is temporary. God is not surprised. God is not absent. God is not cruel. Scripture does not tell us not to grieve. It tells us not to grieve as those without hope (1 Thessalonians 4:13 NIV). Hope does not eliminate tears; it anchors them.

Shock is a bridge, not a residence. You cannot remain at this intersection forever. Grief will unfold in stages. Emotion will deepen. Questions may surface. But this first truth must be secured: God is present. Eternity is real. Christ has conquered death. Everything else flows from there.

# CHAPTER 3

## Denial and Numbness: When Reality Feels Distant

After the initial shock settles, another experience often follows — denial or emotional numbness. For many believers, this stage feels confusing and even shameful. You may wonder why you are not crying anymore. You may question why you feel strangely calm. You may move through necessary tasks — paperwork, arrangements, conversations — almost mechanically. Then the guilt appears. "Why don't I feel more?" "Did I not love deeply enough?" These thoughts are common, but they are not accurate.

Denials are not dishonest. It is protection. The mind absorbs overwhelming pain in portions. God designed the human nervous system with limits. If the full weight of loss were to descend all at once, it could crush the heart. Numbness is often mercy in disguise. It allows you to function when functioning is necessary.

Spiritually, this stage can feel like an autopilot. You attend services. You hear Scripture. You pray familiar prayers. Yet everything feels slightly distant. This does not mean your faith has diminished. It means your emotions are catching up to reality. Faith is not measured by the intensity of feeling. Faith is measured by direction — where you turn when feeling fades.

Some believers fear numbness because they equate emotional expressions with spiritual health. But Scripture shows us varied responses to loss. Abraham mourned Sarah. David wept openly. Others grieved quietly. The expression differed, but love was real. There is no biblical command requiring visible emotion to validate grief.

At this stage, another temptation arises: to lock grief away permanently. Because numbness can feel safer than pain, some attempt to remain there. They avoid quiet moments. They stay constantly busy. They refuse conversations that may stir emotion. But denial is meant to be transitional, not permanent. When ignored too long, buried grief often resurfaces irritability, anxiety, physical symptoms, or spiritual dryness.

The corrective here is gentle exposure. Allow yourself small moments of remembrance. Look at the photograph briefly. Speak their name. Pray honestly. You do not have to force tears. You do not have to manufacture emotions. But you must allow reality to settle gradually.

During this stage, guard against comparing your grief to others. One sibling may cry daily. Another may remain composed. One friend may withdraw. Another may talk constantly. Grief is deeply personal because love is deeply personal. Comparison only produces unnecessary shame.

Return again to an eternal perspective. The distance you feel emotionally does not change the spiritual reality. Christ remains risen. God remains sovereign. Heaven remains secure. Even when you feel detached, truth is not.

If you sense that numbness is lingering beyond its protective purpose — if months pass and you feel nothing at all — it may be wise to seek counsel. Serious grief requires serious listeners. Not everyone is equipped to walk through prolonged sorrow. A trained counselor, pastor experienced in crisis care, or qualified support group can help guide you forward safely. Seeking help is not a weakness; it is wisdom.

Denial and numbness are stages, not destinations. They are evidence that the heart is adjusting to a new reality. Be patient with yourself. Do not shame your process. But do not build a home in emotional avoidance. God walks with you through this stage as surely as He does through tears.

You are not faithless because you feel distant. You are human. And humanity, redeemed in Christ, is still learning how to carry eternity inside fragile flesh.

# CHAPTER 4

## Anger Without Sin

Anger is one of the most misunderstood stages of grief, especially among believers. We are often more comfortable admitting sadness than anger. Sadness feels tender and acceptable. Anger feels dangerous and unspiritual. Yet anger is a natural response to loss. When death takes someone we love, something inside us recognizes that it is not the way things were meant to be. Death is an enemy. Scripture calls it the last enemy to be destroyed. It is not unnatural to feel anger when confronted with it.

Anger in grief can be directed in many directions. You may feel anger toward doctors, toward circumstances, toward family members, toward yourself, or even toward the one who died. You may feel anger toward God. This does not make you faithless. It makes you human. The question is not whether anger will surface. The question is what you will do with it.

There is a difference between feeling anger and living in it. Ephesians 4:26 reminds us, "Be ye angry, and sin not" in the King James Version, and in the New International Version, "In your anger do not sin." Scripture does not deny anger. It regulates it. Anger becomes sinful when it turns into accusation, bitterness, revenge, or hardened resentment. Righteous anger acknowledges injustice and loss. Sinful anger seeks to wound, punish, or withdraw from God.

Many believers struggle silently with anger toward God after a death. They may never say it aloud, but inside they ask why. Why now? Why this way? Why not healing? Why not more time? These questions are not uncommon in Scripture. The Psalms are filled with honest cries. But biblical lament moves toward trust, not away from it. It brings frustration into God's presence instead of using frustration as a reason to abandon Him.

If you feel anger rising, acknowledge it honestly before the Lord. Suppressed anger does not disappear. It redirects. It may surface as irritability with loved ones, harsh words, spiritual withdrawal, or physical tension. Naming anger reduces its power. Saying, "Lord, I am angry," is not rebellion. It is transparency. But follow it with surrender. Ask Him to purify it, to prevent it from turning into bitterness.

Anger can also mask deeper emotions. Sometimes beneath anger is fear. Beneath fear is sadness. Beneath sadness is love. When someone mattered deeply, the disruption of that relationship shakes the foundation of daily life. Anger can feel stronger and more protective than vulnerability. Yet healing requires access to what is underneath.

In this stage, guard against spiritual pride. Some believers attempt to appear unaffected, believing anger is a sign of weak faith. Others justify harsh behavior because they are grieving. Neither extreme reflects maturity. Grief does not excuse sin. Nor does faith eliminate emotional intensity. Mature faith allows emotion but submits it to Christ.

Physically, anger activates the body's stress response. Heart rate increases. Muscles tighten. Thoughts race. If you notice these symptoms, slow your breathing. Step away from heated conversations. Walk outside. Drink water. Pray slowly. The body often needs calming before the spirit can reflect clearly.

Worship during anger may feel difficult. Songs about goodness may feel distant. Yet this is often when worship is most needed. Not as denial, but as recalibration. You may not feel ready to declare victory, but you can whisper dependence. Even saying the name of Jesus slowly can soften the edge of rage.

Remember that Christ Himself overturned tables in the temple when confronted with corruption. Anger in defense of what is holy is not sin. But He did not sin in His anger. His anger was controlled, purposeful, and free from malice. Let Him be your model.

Anger in grief is a stage, not a destination. If nurtured, it becomes bitterness. If surrendered, it becomes clarity. Clarity reminds you that death is wrong, that loss hurts, and that your heart was designed for eternity. That recognition can redirect anger toward longing for the final restoration God promises.

Do not shame yourself for feeling anger. But do not baptize it and call it righteousness without examination. Bring it into the light. Ask God to search your heart. Allow Him to refine what you feel. In doing so, anger becomes another place where eternity reshapes your humanity.

When anger softens, what often remains is sorrow. And sorrow, when anchored in hope, becomes the soil in which healing grows.

Would you like to continue with Bargaining and False Guilt next, or move directly into Depression and the discussion of medication and psychoeducation.

# CHAPTER 5

## Bargaining and False Guilt

After anger begins to settle, the mind often turns inward. It replays conversations. It revisits decisions. It reconstructs timelines. This is the stage often described as bargaining, but for many believers it feels more like self-interrogation. Thoughts begin with two small words that carry enormous weight. If only.

If only I had noticed sooner. If only I had called more often. If only I had insisted on a second opinion. If only I had prayed harder. If only I had been there that day.

Bargaining attempts to rewrite what has already occurred. It is the mind's effort to regain control in a situation where control was never fully ours. In grief, this can become spiritually tangled. Some begin to believe that their faith was insufficient. Others fear that God withheld intervention because of hidden failure. False guilt can quietly take root and grow into shame.

It is important to say this clearly. You are not sovereign. God is. Psalm 139 reminds us that our days are written before one of them comes to be. That truth is not meant to silence sorrow, but to relieve you of imagined responsibility. Hindsight feels powerful because it sees clearly after the fact. But you did not possess that clarity in the moment. You acted with the knowledge and strength you had at the time.

There is a difference between true conviction and false guilt. Conviction identifies a specific wrong and leads to repentance and peace. False guilt is vague, relentless, and never satisfied. It keeps moving the target. Even if you confess one imagined failure, another appears. This is not the voice of the Holy Spirit. It is the mind trying to control what cannot be undone.

For believers, bargaining can also take a spiritual form. You may promise to live differently, to serve more, to give more, if only the pain will ease. While growth can emerge from grief, transformation born from desperation is different from transformation born from surrender. God does not negotiate with loss. He redeems it.

If you find yourself trapped in repeated what-if thinking, pause and ask whether the thought leads you closer to peace or deeper into torment. If it produces only self-condemnation, it is not fruitful. Romans 8:1 declares that there is now no condemnation for those who are in Christ Jesus. Grief may expose regret, but it does not revoke grace.

This stage requires gentle but firm corrcction. You can review the past to learn, but you cannot relive it to change it. Release what you cannot alter. Pray honestly. If there are real apologies that were never spoken, speak them to God. If forgiveness needs to be extended, extend it. But refuse to carry responsibility for outcomes that belonged to God alone.

False guilt can exhaust the body and spirit. It interferes with sleep and fuels anxiety. When you notice yourself circling the same mental path repeatedly, redirect intentionally. Read Scripture aloud. Call a trusted counselor. Write down the thought and answer it with truth. Healing requires confronting distortion with clarity.

Bargaining feels active, but it keeps you suspended in the past. Eternity calls you forward. Trust that God's sovereignty was present even when your understanding was limited. His purposes are not fragile. They are not undone by human imperfection.

When false guilt loosens its grip, what remains is grief unburdened by self-accusation. That grief can then be carried honestly without the added weight of imagined failure.

# CHAPTER 6

## Depression, Despair, and the Responsibility of Care

As grief deepens, sadness may intensify. Energy decreases. Motivation fades. Tears may come unexpectedly, or they may not come at all. This stage often brings confusion because believers are unsure how to distinguish between grief and depression. It is important to approach this with maturity and balance.

Grief and clinical depression are not identical, though they can overlap. Grief tends to move in waves. Even in sorrow, moments of light can break through. Depression often feels more constant and heavy, marked by persistent hopelessness, loss of pleasure in nearly all activities, changes in appetite or sleep, and sometimes thoughts of self-harm. If these symptoms become severe or prolonged, professional evaluation is not a sign of weak faith. It is wisdom.

Medication in such cases may be appropriate. Antidepressants can stabilize chemical imbalances and reduce dangerous symptoms. For someone experiencing suicidal ideation or severe impairment, medical support can be life-preserving. Taking prescribed medication under supervision is not a betrayal of trust in God. It is an acknowledgment that God works through physicians and treatment as well as through prayer.

However, medication is not transformation. It may stabilize mood, but it does not teach coping skills, process trauma, or rebuild spiritual perspective. This is where psychoeducation becomes vital. Understanding what grief does to the brain and body reduces fear. Learning that disrupted sleep, irritability, and difficulty concentrating are common responses to loss can provide relief. Knowledge removes unnecessary panic.

There is responsibility in this stage. You must care for your mind as intentionally as you care for your spirit. Isolation prolongs despair. Structure provides stability. Returning gradually to routine can protect against rumination. Taking extended time away from all responsibility may feel appealing, but prolonged withdrawal can deepen depression. Grief needs space, but it also needs rhythm.

Despair differs from sadness. Sadness acknowledges loss. Despair abandons hope. Scripture consistently confronts despair not by denying pain, but by reminding the believer of God's character. Elijah once collapsed under exhaustion and asked to die. God did not shame him. He fed him. He allowed him to rest. Then He spoke gently and redirected him. This pattern matters. Physical care and spiritual redirection worked together.

During this stage, guard against allowing grief to become identity. You are grieving, but you are not defined solely by grief. You are still a child of God. Depression whispers that nothing will improve. Eternity answers that this is not the end of the story.

If you ever experience thoughts of self-harm or persistent hopelessness, seek immediate help from a qualified professional or crisis resource. Serious suffering requires serious listeners. Not everyone is equipped to provide life-saving guidance. Choose counsel wisely.

This chapter calls for maturity. Accept help if needed. Learn what is happening biologically. Submit your emotions to God daily. Eat, sleep, move, and speak with someone safely. Worship even when it feels mechanical. Transformation rarely happens in a single dramatic moment. It unfolds through steady obedience.

Depression does not mean your faith has failed. It means your humanity is under strain. Faith during this stage may feel quiet and small, but small faith anchored in a great God is still powerful. Care for your mind responsibly. Care for your body intentionally. Care for your spirit faithfully. Healing often emerges not from one decision, but from consistent stewardship over time.

There are seasons in grief when strength feels depleted, and even structured discipline feels difficult. In those moments, prayer becomes simple. Sometimes it is reduced to a single plea — Lord, do it for me. That cry is not weakness. It is surrender. It acknowledges that while responsibility matters, ultimate restoration belongs to God. Dependence does not negate effort. It completes it.

We can continue next with The Body as Temple in Grief and When Grief Becomes Identity or move into When You Have No One to Talk To.

# CHAPTER 7

## Acceptance: Anchored Hope

Acceptance is often described as the final stage of grief, but it is not the disappearance of sorrow. It is the surrender of resistance. It is the moment when you stop arguing with reality and begin living within it.

Acceptance does not mean you like what happened. It does not mean you would not change it if you could. It does not mean you no longer miss the person you loved. It means you acknowledge that the loss is real and that life must now be lived differently.

For believers, acceptance is deeply spiritual. It is not passive resignation. It is an active trust.

There comes a point in grief when the heart grows tired of fighting what cannot be undone. The mind has replayed the past. The emotions have surged and receded. The questions have been asked. And slowly, quietly, the soul says; this is my new reality.

That moment is sacred.

Acceptance is where grief begins to integrate instead of dominating. You still remember. You still feel. But the loss no longer controls every thought. It becomes part of your story without consuming the entire narrative.

Spiritually, acceptance aligns closely with surrender. Not surrender to death but surrender to God's sovereignty. You may never understand why. You may never see the full picture this side of eternity. But you choose to trust without accusation.

Jesus in Gethsemane modeled this tension. He expressed His anguish honestly yet concluded with surrender. Not my will, but Thine is done. Acceptance does not silence emotion. It aligns it.

Acceptance also restores forward movement. You begin making plans again without guilt. You reengage with life without feeling betrayal. You laugh and do not immediately apologize for it. Joy returns quietly at first. Then steadily.

This stage often surprises people. They expect a dramatic breakthrough. Instead, acceptance usually arrives gently. It feels less like celebration and more like stability.

You wake up one day and realize the pain is no longer sharp in the same way. You can speak their name without your chest tightening. You can think about the future without feeling disloyal.

That is acceptance.

Acceptance also carries eternal clarity. You understand that death is not ultimate. You understand that separation in Christ is temporary. You understand that your time remains purposeful.

Hope becomes less emotional and more settled. It no longer needs to be forced. It rests quietly beneath your days.

Acceptance does not mean grief never returns. It may revisit you in waves during anniversaries or milestones. But it does not overwhelm you as before. It moves through rather than over you.

For the believer, acceptance is anchored hope. It says:

God is still God.
Christ is still risen.
Heaven is still real.
My calling still remains.

Acceptance is not the end of love. It is the beginning of living faithfully with love carried forward.

You have not forgotten.
You have not betrayed me.
You have not minimized.

You have trusted me.

And that trust becomes the steady ground beneath your remaining years.

# CHAPTER 8

## The Body as Temple in Grief

Grief is spiritual, but it is not only spiritual. It is emotional, neurological, and physical. Many believers attempt to process loss entirely through prayer and Scripture while quietly neglecting their bodies. Over time, this imbalance weakens resilience. The body and spirit are not enemies. They are intertwined. When one is neglected, the other struggles.

Scripture reminds us that the body is the temple of the Holy Spirit. That truth does not disappear in seasons of sorrow. In fact, it becomes more urgent. Grief elevates stress hormones, disrupts digestion, alters sleep cycles, and weakens immunity. Headaches, muscle tension, fatigue, and chest tightness are common. These are not signs that you lack faith. They are signs that your system is under strain.

Some believers dismiss physical care during grief, believing it to be secondary or even indulgent. Yet stewardship of the body is obedient. Eating regularly stabilizes mood. Hydration improves cognitive clarity. Sleep restores emotional regulation. Gentle movement reduces stress chemicals. These are not worldly techniques. They are practical expressions of wisdom.

There is also danger in the opposite direction. Some attempt to escape grief by overworking the body, pushing themselves relentlessly, or numbing through unhealthy habits. Overexertion, substance misuse, or emotional suppression disguised as discipline can delay healing. Balance is required. The body needs care, not punishment, and not neglect.

Taking time off work may be necessary initially, but extended withdrawal from all responsibility can unintentionally deepen isolation. Structure provides grounding. Routine reminds the mind that life continues. A gradual return to daily rhythm often protects against rumination. Grief needs space, but it also needs boundaries. Without them, sorrow can expand unchecked.

Caring for the body during grief is not an attempt to outrun pain. It is preparation to endure it. When the body is supported, the spirit has greater capacity to process truth. Elijah's experience illustrates this well. When he collapsed under despair, God did not begin with a lecture. He provided rest and food. Physical restoration preceded spiritual instruction.

Pay attention to warning signs. Persistent insomnia, significant weight change, ongoing exhaustion, or reliance on alcohol or medication without supervision require attention. Serious strain requires serious care. Seeking medical or therapeutic support is not a denial of faith. It is recognition that God often works through trained hands.

When sorrow tempts you to neglect yourself, remember that your body still belongs to God. You are not called to honor the deceased by destroying your health. Nor are you called to prove strength through endurance alone. The temple must be maintained.

Grief touches every system of the body. Therefore, healing must involve the whole person. Eat with intention. Rest without guilt. Move gently. Seek help when needed. These actions do not compete with spirituality. They support it. The more stable the body, the steadier the soul.

# CHAPTER 9

## When Grief Becomes Identity

There is a subtle shift that can occur in prolonged grief. What began as a season slowly becomes a label. Instead of saying, I am grieving, the mind begins to believe, I am grief. The loss becomes central not only to memory, but to identity. Conversations return repeatedly to the same pain. Decisions revolve around preserving sorrow. Healing feels betrayal.

This stage requires careful discernment. Grief is honorable. Mourning is biblical. Jesus declared blessed are those who mourn. But mourning in Scripture was a season. Sackcloth was worn, but it was eventually removed. Ashes marked sorrow, but they were not permanent attire. When grief becomes enthroned instead of acknowledged, it begins to reshape identity in unhealthy ways.

One danger in this stage is idolization of loss. The relationship that ended becomes the defining feature of existence. The pain itself feels sacred. Moving forward may feel disloyal. Some fear that healing means forgetting. Others believe joy dishonors the one who died. These thoughts feel noble, but they are not accurate.

Love is not measured by perpetual sorrow. Love is honored by living faithfully with the time that remains. The person you lost does not require your lifelong paralysis as proof of devotion. Eternity assures reunion. That promise frees you to live now without guilt.

Grief as identity can also distort spiritual focus. Instead of centering life on Christ, sorrow becomes the organizing force. Scripture, prayer, and worship may begin to revolve exclusively around loss. While God welcomes grief, He does not intend for it to replace Him as the core of your being.

If you notice that months or years have passed and grief feels unchanged in intensity, or if it prevents engagement with relationships, work, or purpose, it may be time for intentional intervention. Complicated grief is real. It requires structured care. Counseling can help untangle attachment from identity and restore healthy movement forward.

The goal is not forgetting. The goal is integration. The memory of the one you loved becomes part of your story without consuming the entire narrative. You can speak their name without collapsing. You can remember without reliving. You can feel sorrow without losing direction.

Christ remains your identity. Not loss. Not pain. Not widow. Not orphan. Not bereaved parent. Those describe experiences, not essence. Your essence remains anchored in being a child of God.

In moments when identity feels fragile, worship can restore clarity. Tasha Cobbs Leonard's declaration, "You know my name," reminds the grieving believer that before loss altered your title, God already knew you personally. He does not define you by your sorrow. He does not confuse you with your pain. You are known — fully, intimately, intentionally. Grief may shift roles, but it cannot erase divine recognition.

Grief is a chapter, not the title of your life. When it attempts to define you permanently, return to eternity. The story is larger than this loss. Redemption is still unfolding. Joy may return quietly at first, but it is not betrayal. It is evidence that resurrection power continues to work within you.

We can continue next with Spiritual Crisis and Trust Without Accusation and then When You Have No One to Talk To, or shift toward Wise Counsel and Serious Listeners.

# CHAPTER 10

## Spiritual Crisis and Trust Without Accusation

There comes a point in grief when the struggle is no longer primarily emotional. It becomes theological. Not in the academic sense, but in the deeply personal sense. What you believe about God is pressed, stretched, and examined under the weight of loss. This is spiritual crisis. It does not mean abandonment of faith. It means faith is being tested in the fire of reality.

You may find yourself asking questions you never expected to ask. Why did God allow this. Why did He not intervene. Why did healing not come. Why did prayer seem unanswered. These questions surface naturally when eternity collides with mortality. The danger is not in the questions themselves. The danger is in the posture behind them.

Scripture is filled with lament. The Psalms cry out with confusion and sorrow. Job questioned deeply. Even Christ, in His humanity, cried out from the cross. But biblical lament brings pain toward God. Accusation pushes God away. There is a difference between saying, I do not understand, and declaring, You were wrong.

Trust without accusation is mature faith. It acknowledges limited understanding while affirming God's unchanging character. You may not understand His timing. You may not see His purposes. But you anchor yourself in who He has revealed Himself to be. Holy. Just. Merciful. Faithful.

Worship grounded in God's character steadies the soul when explanations are absent. In "Because of Who You Are," Vicki Yohe declares trust not based on circumstance, but on identity — Jehovah Jireh, Jehovah Nissi, Lord of all. When grief tempts you to question what God has allowed, return to who He is. His character does not fluctuate with your pain. His nature remains constant, even when outcomes do not.

Spiritual crisis often reveals hidden assumptions. Some believers quietly expect that obedience guarantees protection from severe loss. When tragedy comes, it feels like betrayal. Yet Scripture never promises exemption from sorrow. It promises presence in sorrow. The cross itself stands as proof that suffering is not evidence of divine neglect.

During this stage, guard your inputs carefully. Well-meaning voices may offer explanations that are simplistic or harsh. Avoid theology that blames the grieving. Avoid interpretations that suggest secret sin as the cause of tragedy. Such conclusions wound rather than heal. Seek counsel rooted in Scripture and compassion.

You may also feel distance in prayer. Words may seem empty. Worship may feel mechanical. Continue anyway. Faith during spiritual crisis is not loud. It is steady. It is choosing to remain in relationship with God even when emotions fluctuate. The absence of feeling does not equal the absence of God.

If anger resurfaces during this stage, return to surrender. Say honestly what you feel but refuse to define God by your pain. Remember the resurrection. The same God who allowed the crucifixion also raised Christ from the grave. What appears final is not ultimate.

Spiritual crisis refines belief. It strips away shallow assumptions and forces deeper roots. If you allow it, this stage will not destroy faith. It will mature it. Trust without accusation does not mean silence. It means reverence. It means acknowledging mystery without abandoning confidence in God's goodness.

There are moments in grief when explanation is unavailable and emotion is unsettled. In those moments, worship that exalts God's supremacy can recalibrate the heart. VaShawn Mitchell's declaration, "Nobody greater than You," is not emotional denial. It is theological alignment. It is the decision to affirm that even when understanding fails, God's authority does not. No circumstance outranks Him. No loss dethrones Him. No sorrow diminishes His sovereignty.

Grief may shake your understanding, but it cannot overturn eternity. Anchor there. Even when you do not understand His hand, trust His heart.

# CHAPTER 11

## When You Have No One to Talk To

One of the most painful realities in grief is isolation. In the first days after a loss, support often surrounds you. Calls come. Messages arrive. Meals are delivered. But as weeks pass, the world resumes its rhythm. Others return to routine. You may still feel suspended.

Loneliness in grief is common. Some withdraw intentionally because conversation feels exhausting. Others remain silent because they believe they must appear strong. Some try to speak but discover that not everyone is equipped to listen. Serious grief requires serious listeners. Not every friend, family member, or acquaintance has the capacity to handle life-altering sorrow.

It is important to recognize the difference between companionship and qualified support. Companionship offers presence. Qualified support offers guidance. Both matter. But when grief becomes heavy, confusing, or prolonged, presence alone may not be enough. You need someone trained to navigate despair, guilt, trauma, or complicated attachment.

There is no shame in seeking professional counseling. A licensed therapist, grief counselor, or pastor experienced in crisis care can provide structured help. They can ask the questions others avoid. They can challenge distorted thinking gently. They can offer tools that protect against destructive patterns.

If you feel that you have no one safe to speak with, take deliberate steps to change that. Research local grief groups. Contact counseling centers. Speak with trusted church leadership and ask specifically about training and experience. Not everyone who offers spiritual advice is prepared for life-saving conversations. Choose carefully.

Isolation intensifies distorted thinking. When thoughts remain unspoken, they can grow unchecked. Saying them aloud often reduces their power. If you cannot access immediate in-person support, consider reputable crisis lines or virtual counseling services. In moments of severe distress or thoughts of self-harm, seek emergency assistance immediately. Your life remains valuable.

You are not meant to carry grief alone. Even Christ asked His disciples to remain awake with Him in His hour of sorrow. Human support does not replace God's presence. It reflects it. God often works through people.

If pride or fear prevents you from reaching out, examine that gently. Strength is not silence. Strength is appropriate vulnerability. It is recognizing when you need help and seeking it responsibly.

There may be seasons when you feel misunderstood. Continue searching for safe spaces. The right listener can make a profound difference. Healing accelerates when truth is spoken in compassionate environments.

Grief can isolate, but it does not have to imprison. Take one step toward connection. Send one message. Make one call. Schedule one appointment. Eternity does not require you to endure suffering in isolation. God's design includes community.

We can move next into Wise Counsel and Dangerous Advice followed by Living Forward Without Betrayal, or begin shaping the concluding arc of the book toward hope and eternal perspective.

**Serious suffering requires serious listeners.**

# CHAPTER 12

## Wise Counsel and Dangerous Advice

As grief progresses, the voices around you begin to matter more than you may realize. Some voices will steady you. Others, though well intentioned, may confuse or wound you. Discernment becomes essential. Not every person who speaks into your sorrow is equipped to guide you through it.

There is a difference between comfort and counsel. Comfort offers empathy and presence. Counsel offers direction and correction when needed. Both are valuable, but they are not interchangeable. A friend may sit with you faithfully yet lack the training to navigate trauma, depression, or spiritual crisis. A pastor may offer Scripture but may not be experienced in complicated grief dynamics. Wisdom lies in recognizing what kind of help you need and seeking it intentionally.

Dangerous advice often sounds spiritual. Statements such as "You just need more faith," or "Stop dwelling on it," or "Everything happens for a reason," may silence you rather than strengthen you. These phrases, though sometimes spoken with kindness, can minimize real pain. They may also create shame, as if continued sorrow indicates spiritual failure. Grief does not disappear on command. It must be processed with patience and truth.

Another form of dangerous advice is the encouragement to isolate or suppress. Some may suggest that talking too much about the deceased prevents healing. Others may insist that constant busyness is the best remedy. While balance is important, forced silence or endless distraction often delay necessary emotional work. Healing requires honesty, not avoidance.

Wise counsel, by contrast, combines compassion with clarity. It listens without rushing. It corrects gently when thinking becomes distorted. It respects both Scripture and psychological realities. Wise counsel reminds you of hope without denying sorrow. It does not shame tears, nor does it excuse destructive behavior.

If someone consistently leaves you feeling judged, confused, or diminished after conversations about your grief, reconsider the influence of that voice. Protecting your heart is not arrogance. It is stewardship. Proverbs reminds us that in the multitude of counselors there is safety, but the quality of counsel matters more than the quantity.

In this stage, you may need to limit exposure to certain conversations. You are not required to explain your healing process to everyone. Nor are you obligated to receive every opinion offered. Grief is sacred ground. Guard it carefully.

Seek those who combine spiritual maturity with emotional intelligence. Seek those who are not threatened by your questions. Seek those who understand that faith and psychology are not enemies. When you find such counsel, remain teachable. Even correction, when offered in love, can accelerate healing.

Your grief journey will be influenced by the voices you allow. Choose them wisely. Not everyone is equipped with life saving answers. Some offer comfort. A few offer guidance. Discern the difference.

# CHAPTER 13

## Living Forward Without Betrayal

One of the quiet fears in grief is the fear of moving forward. At some point, laughter returns briefly. A day passes without tears. You begin to make plans again. And suddenly guilt appears. Am I forgetting. Am I betraying their memory. Is it wrong to feel normal again.

This stage is subtle but significant. Healing can feel like disloyalty. Especially in deep love, sorrow feels like proof of devotion. If the intensity decreases, it may seem as though love has weakened. This is not true. Love does not require perpetual suffering to remain authentic.

Eternity reframes this fear. For the believer, separation is temporary. The one you loved is not erased. They are not diminished by your continued living. Your forward movement does not dishonor them. It honors the life God has entrusted to you.

Living forward does not mean leaving the past behind. It means integrating it. You carry memories with gratitude rather than paralysis. You speak their name without collapsing. You allow joy to coexist with remembrance. This balance reflects maturity.

There will be moments when grief resurfaces unexpectedly. Anniversaries, holidays, familiar songs, or certain places may trigger renewed sorrow. This does not mean you have regressed. It means love remains present. Grief does not disappear entirely. It changes shape.

Some believers fear that joy after loss is inappropriate. Yet Scripture repeatedly affirms that sorrow and joy can coexist. Weeping may endure for a night, but joy comes in the morning. Morning does not deny the night. It follows it.

As you move forward, purpose often begins to reemerge. You may feel called to serve differently, to support others walking through loss, or to deepen spiritual disciplines. Let growth unfold naturally. Do not force transformation. Allow God to shape new direction gradually.

Living forward also requires practical engagement. Reestablish routine. Reconnect with relationships. Resume responsibilities at a measured pace. Structure supports stability. Isolation prolongs stagnation. Engage life intentionally without rushing.

If you sense that fear is holding you back from necessary steps, bring that honestly before God. Ask Him to release you from guilt that He has not assigned. Remember that your identity remains anchored in Christ, not in loss. The story of your life did not end when theirs did.

Living forward without betrayal is an act of trust. It says that God's plan for you continues. It acknowledges that eternity holds reunion. It allows you to walk toward the future without abandoning the past.

Grief brought you to a crossroads. Eternity invites you onward.

# CHAPTER 14

## Hope That Outlives the Funeral

There is a quiet moment after the funeral when reality settles differently. The service has ended. The flowers fade. The calls slow down. The house feels still. This is often when grief deepens. Public support gives way to private processing. It is here, in the quiet, that hope must become more than a phrase spoken at a service. It must become an anchor.

Christian hope is not optimism. It is not pretending that loss is smaller than it is. Hope is confidence rooted in the character of God and the promise of resurrection. It does not deny sorrow. It sustains you within it. The funeral proclaims eternity publicly. The weeks after require believing it personally.

In these quieter days, the absence feels sharper. You notice routines that no longer exist. Conversations that will not happen again. Spaces that remain empty. The temptation here is subtle despair. Not loud, dramatic hopelessness, but a quiet heaviness that asks what now. What does life look like without them. How do I rebuild my meaning?

Scripture does not shy away from this tension. The early church grieved, yet they grieved differently. They believed that death was not final. First Thessalonians remind believers not to grieve as those without hope. It does not instruct the elimination of grief. It commands the preservation of hope.

Hope after the funeral requires intentional reinforcement. You must remind yourself of what you believe even when emotions lag behind. Read Scripture aloud. Return to promises of resurrection. Meditate on passages describing eternal reunion. Let your theology minister to your heart.

This stage may also require renewed community engagement. Grief thrives in isolation. While solitude can be healthy briefly, prolonged withdrawal deepens heaviness. Attend worship even if you feel detached. Participate even if you feel quiet. Community strengthens perspective.

Worship music may take on new meaning during this season. Songs about victory over death are no longer abstract. They are personal. When a worship leader sings about chains breaking, remember that death's ultimate chain has already been broken through Christ. Let that truth recalibrate your outlook.

Hope does not eliminate tears months after loss. It changes their context. You may cry and still believe. You may miss deeply and still trust fully. Mature hope allows both realities to coexist.

As days turn into months, allow yourself to rebuild routines gradually. Create new patterns without erasing old memories. Celebrate milestones with remembrance rather than avoidance. Grief will revisit you in waves, but waves eventually recede.

The funeral marked an ending on earth. It did not mark an ending in eternity. Anchor yourself there. Hope outlives the ceremony. It outlives the casket. It outlives the grave. Because Christ lives, hope lives.

# CHAPTER 15

## Preparing for Your Own Eternity

Grief does something few other experiences can do. It confronts you with your own mortality. As you stand at the crossroads of eternity for someone else, you are reminded that one day others will stand there for you. This realization can be unsettling, but it is also clarifying.

Death is certain. Timing is not. Scripture teaches that life is a vapor, appearing briefly and then vanishing. This is not meant to produce fear. It is meant to produce wisdom. When confronted honestly, mortality sharpens priorities. It reveals what truly matters.

Preparing for your own eternity does not mean living in dread. It means living intentionally. Examine your relationship with God. Strengthen daily spiritual disciplines. Repair strained relationships while time remains. Speak forgiveness sooner rather than later. Express love clearly and often.

It also means making practical arrangements. Clarify your wishes. Communicate them responsibly. Preparation is not a lack of faith. It is stewardship. It relieves loved ones of unnecessary confusion during future grief.

Spiritually, preparation involves assurance. As a believer, anchor yourself in the promises of Christ. Salvation is not earned through performance. It is received through faith. Let that assurance quiet anxiety. Eternity for the Christian is not uncertainty. It is promise.

Reflect on how you want to be remembered. Not in reputation alone, but in character. Grief reveals the impact of a life. Live in such a way that your legacy reflects faithfulness, integrity, and love.

Preparing for eternity also deepens compassion. When you recognize the brevity of life, you hold others more gently. You argue less. You forgive faster. You prioritize presence over trivial pursuits.

This final stage of reflection is not morbid. It is mature. It completes the journey from standing at someone else's grave to examining your own spiritual readiness. It aligns daily living with eternal reality.

The crossroads of eternity is not only encountered at death. It is encountered in life when you choose what matters most. Let grief refine you. Let eternity focus you. Live now with the confidence that death is not defeat but transition for those in Christ.

Your journey through grief has led you here. From shock to sorrow, from anger to surrender, from isolation to renewed hope. Eternity has remained constant throughout. Carry that constancy forward.

If you would like, we can now craft the final concluding chapter to tie the entire book together with a strong, spiritually resonant closing.

# CHAPTER 16

## Until We Meet Again

Every journey through grief eventually arrives at a quiet resolve. Not the resolve that says the pain is gone, but the resolve that says the pain will not rule. The tears may still come. The memories may still surface unexpectedly. Certain days may still carry weight. But something has shifted. Eternity has settled deeper into the heart.

Grief changes you. It strips illusions of permanence. It reveals how fragile life truly is. It forces you to confront what you believe about God, about death, about reunion, and about hope. If you have walked honestly through these chapters, you have not avoided sorrow. You have faced it in the light of Scripture and eternity.

There is comfort in remembering that for the believer, goodbye is not permanent. It is until we meet again. The separation is real, but it is not final. Christ's resurrection is not symbolic encouragement. It is historical promise. Because He lives, death does not have the final word.

This does not erase longing. You will still wish for another conversation, another embrace, another shared moment. That longing is not weakness. It is evidence that you were created for continuity, not separation. Eternity is woven into your design. Loss feels unnatural because in God's original design, it was.

In this closing season of grief, guard your heart from two extremes. Do not pretend that nothing changed. And do not allow the change to define everything. You can acknowledge the permanent absence while embracing present responsibility. You can honor memory while pursuing purpose.

The life you still have is sacred. It is not secondary because someone else's life ended. God's plan for you did not conclude at their passing. The same Lord who walked with you through sorrow continues to walk with you forward. Grief may have slowed you, but it has not disqualified you.

As you move forward, consider how this journey has reshaped your compassion. You now understand sorrow differently. You recognize quiet pain in others more quickly. Perhaps your calling will include walking beside someone else at their crossroads. Suffering often deepens ministry. What wounded you may one day equip you.

When waves of grief return, and they will, do not interpret them as failure. Healing is not linear. It unfolds in layers. Some days will feel strong. Others may feel tender again. In both, God remains steady. Return to the truths that carried you from the beginning. God is present. Eternity is real. Christ has conquered death.

Until we meet again is not a phrase of denial. It is a declaration of faith. It rests on the promise that for those in Christ, reunion is certain. Let that promise soften your sorrow and strengthen your endurance.

One day, grief will cease entirely. One day, tears will be wiped away. One day, death will be no more. Until that day, live faithfully. Love deeply. Forgive quickly. Worship consistently. Prepare wisely.

You stood at the crossroads of eternity and did not turn away. You faced loss with honesty and faith. Carry that faith forward.

Until we meet again.

# CHAPTER 17

## Benediction at the Crossroads

If you have come this far, you have not avoided grief. You have walked through it. You have allowed sorrow to speak, but you have not allowed it to reign. You have examined anger without baptizing it, guilt without surrendering to it, depression without surrendering hope. You have confronted spiritual crisis without abandoning trust. You have stood at the crossroads of eternity and chosen faith.

This final chapter is not instruction. It is blessing.

Grief has a way of stripping life down to essentials. It removes illusion. It exposes fragility. It clarifies what matters. In doing so, it offers something unexpected. Depth. Depth of compassion. Depth of prayer. Depth of dependence on God. What once may have been theological language has now become lived experience.

You now know something you did not know before. You know how silence feels after a funeral. You know how memory can ache. You know how faith must sometimes be chosen rather than felt. That knowledge does not weaken you. It matures you.

May you carry forward what grief has refined rather than what it has wounded. May you remember that sorrow visited you, but it did not claim you. Your identity remains anchored in Christ. Not in loss.

Not in absence. Not in what was taken. But in what was secured eternally.

When questions resurface, return to the cross. When loneliness rises, return to community. When exhaustion lingers, return to stewardship of your body. When doubt whispers, return to Scripture. The disciplines that sustained you in grief will sustain you in life.

There will be days ahead that feel unexpectedly joyful. Receive them without guilt. There will be days that feel tender again. Meet them with patience. Healing does not erase memory. It reorders it. Memory becomes gratitude rather than only ache.

Do not fear living fully again. Your capacity to love remains. Your capacity to serve remains. Your calling remains. The one you lost does not require your stagnation as tribute. Honor them by walking faithfully in the time that remains yours.

As you prepare for your own eternity, live in such a way that when your day comes, those you leave behind will grieve with hope. Model what you have learned. Speak openly about eternity. Clarify your wishes. Strengthen your faith daily. Leave a legacy of trust.

The crossroads of eternity is not a single moment. It is encountered repeatedly throughout life in choices, priorities, and perspective. Let grief have taught you to choose what lasts.

May the peace of God, which surpasses understanding, guard your heart and mind. May hope remain steady. May worship remain sincere. May your life reflect the certainty that death is not defeat for those in Christ.

Walk forward now. Not untouched by sorrow, but transformed by it. Not untouched by tears, but anchored in promise. The journey continues.

And eternity awaits.

# FINAL CHARGE

If you are holding this book in a season of grief, know this: you have not been abandoned. Not by God. Not by eternity. Not by hope.

You have walked through shock. You have wrestled with anger. You have confronted guilt. You have endured waves of sadness. You have questioned quietly. You have searched for steady ground. And through every stage, one truth has remained unshaken: God has not moved.

Grief may have altered your daily life, but it has not altered God's character. He is still faithful. He is still sovereign. He is still near to the brokenhearted.

As you close these pages, do not close the process. Healing is not a single moment of clarity. It is a continued alignment of your heart with eternal truth. Return to Scripture often. Guard your body wisely. Choose your counselors carefully. Refuse to idolize sorrow. Refuse to accuse God. Refuse to surrender hope.

Death brought you to a crossroads. Eternity invites you to walk forward.

Let your life now reflect what grief has taught you. Love intentionally. Speak forgiveness quickly. Worship sincerely. Prepare responsibly. Live aware that this world is temporary and that heaven is not theory.

You are still here. That means purpose remains. Calling remains. Growth remains.

And one day, reunion remains.

Until that day, stand steady in Christ. Walk faithfully. Grieve honestly. Hope confidently.

You are EnRoute.

# CLOSING PRAYER

**Heavenly Father,**

You are the Author of life and the Keeper of eternity. You see what we cannot see. You hold what we cannot hold. And You remain steady when our hearts tremble.

For the one reading these pages in the midst of grief, draw near now. Where sorrow feels heavy, be their strength. Where questions remain unanswered, be their peace. Where anger has surfaced, refine it without condemning. Where guilt lingers, release it with truth. Where depression weighs heavily, bring light, wise counsel, and responsible care.

Remind them that You are not distant from suffering. You entered it. You bore it. You conquered it. The cross was not the end. The grave was not final. Resurrection stands as our assurance that death does not win.

Guard their body as they grieve. Guard their mind as thoughts wander. Guard their spirit from despair. Surround them with serious listeners who speak truth with compassion. Protect them from harmful counsel and from isolation.

Teach them to walk forward without betrayal. Teach them to remember without being consumed. Teach them to live faithfully with eternity in view.

When waves of grief return, anchor them again. When hope feels quiet, steady it. When loneliness whispers, remind them that You remain.

Thank You that for those in Christ, separation is temporary. Thank You that heaven is certain. Thank You that one day tears will be wiped away and death will be no more.

Until that day, help us walk by faith and not by sight at life's final crossroads.

In Jesus' name,
Amen.

# FINAL ANCHOR

You stood at the crossroads of eternity and did not turn away.

You grieved honestly.
You questioned without rebellion.
You felt anger without surrendering to sin.
You carried sorrow without idolizing it.
You sought help without shame.
You trusted without accusing God.

Grief is real, but it is not ultimate.

Death is an enemy, but it is defeated.
Separation is painful, but it is temporary.
Faith may feel small, but it rests on a sovereign God.

You are not drifting.
You are not undone.
You are anchored.

Christ is risen.
Heaven is certain.
Death does not have the final word.

Walk steady.

# ACKNOWLEDGMENTS

No book of this nature is written in isolation.

To the families who have trusted me during their most sacred and vulnerable moments, thank you. Your courage, honesty, and faith in seasons of sorrow have shaped these pages more than you may ever know. I have learned from your endurance, your questions, and your quiet strength.

To colleagues in funeral service who labor with integrity and compassion, your daily commitment to dignity and care continues to inspire me. The calling is sacred, and the responsibility is weighty. May we never forget the humanity behind every service we conduct.

To those in the counseling and pastoral communities who approach grief with both truth and tenderness, thank you for modeling what responsible care looks like. Serious suffering requires serious listeners, and your work reflects that conviction.

To my family and those closest to me, your support and understanding allow this calling to continue. Ministry in grief is demanding, and your steadiness has been a gift.

Most importantly, I acknowledge the Lord Jesus Christ, who stands at the center of every grave and every promise. Without the certainty of resurrection, these words would offer little more than comfort. With Him, they carry hope.

# Acknowledgement

May this book serve those who need steady ground at the crossroads of eternity.

Shawn E. Wells, LFD, BCCC, CGC

# ABOUT THE AUTHOR

Shawn E. Wells, LFD, BCCC, CGC is a Licensed Funeral Director, Board Certified Christian Counselor, and Certified Grief Counselor whose work integrates funeral service, credential literacy, and structured decision-making during life transitions.

With professional experience in both funeral practice and counseling education, Wells emphasizes informed autonomy over emotional reaction. His approach combines psychological awareness, legal clarity, financial responsibility, and disciplined evaluation to strengthen stability at moments of vulnerability.

His original work, *Funeral Service at a Crossroads*, established the foundational framework for what would become the ENROUTE-Rx. As the scope of that work expanded beyond industry structure into broader questions of identity, grief literacy, professional boundaries, and eternal perspective, it was developed into distinct but unified volumes to increase clarity and accessibility for diverse readers.

He is the author of:

- *Funeral Service at a Crossroads*— An examination of the modern funeral profession, addressing industry reform, regulatory oversight, economic pressure, and the preservation of professional dignity.

- *ENROUTE-Rx* — The foundational framework introducing structured evaluation and credential literacy for navigating life transitions.
- *ENROUTE-Rx: Crossroads*— A disciplined question-and-answer guide for individuals and professionals facing grief, legal responsibility, financial decisions, and identity reconstruction.
- *ENROUTE-Rx: At the Crossroads of Eternity*— An exploration of mortality, faith, and eternal accountability within the context of life's decisive moments.

Across his work, Wells maintains a consistent principle: clarity precedes stability. His books are designed for funeral service education, counseling training, ministry development, and interdisciplinary professional instruction.

ENROUTE-RX represents his ongoing commitment to navigating life's most significant crossroads through education, professional insight, and principled structure.

# A 14-DAY THERAPEUTIC GUIDE

Grief requires structure.
Scripture provides direction.
These fourteen-day guides offer one intentional step each day, grounded in biblical truth and practical care.

*(For Anticipatory Grief or the Days Immediately Surrounding Death)*

## Day 1 – Speak What Matters

**Scripture:** *"Let all things be done with charity."* — 1 Corinthians 16:14 (KJV)
Tell them you love them. Remove silence where possible.

## Day 2 – Write a Letter

**Scripture:** *"The memory of the just is blessed."* — Proverbs 10:7 (KJV)
Write gratitude. Write forgiveness. Write blessing.

## Day 3 – Pray Together (If Possible)

**Scripture:** *"Where two or three gather in my name, there am I with them."* — Matthew 18:20 (NIV)
Invite God into the room.

## Day 4 – Prepare Wisely

**Scripture:** *"The prudent see danger and take refuge."* — Proverbs 27:12 (NIV)
Preparation is stewardship, not surrender.

## Day 5 – Share Memories

**Scripture:** *"I remember the days of old; I meditate on all thy works."* — Psalm 143:5 (KJV)
Honor the life that was lived.

## Day 6 – Care for Your Body

**Scripture:** *"Your body is the temple of the Holy Ghost."* — 1 Corinthians 6:19 (KJV)
Eat. Hydrate. Rest. This is obedience.

## Day 7 – Worship Quietly

**Scripture:** *"The Lord is my light and my salvation; whom shall I fear?"* — Psalm 27:1 (KJV)
Let worship steady what words cannot.

## Day 8 – Release False Guilt

**Scripture:** *"There is now no condemnation for those who are in Christ Jesus."* — Romans 8:1 (NIV)
You are not sovereign. God is.

## Day 9 – Identify Support

**Scripture:** *"Bear ye one another's burdens."* — Galatians 6:2 (KJV)
Choose serious listeners.

## Day 10 – Breathe and Be Still

**Scripture:** *"Be still, and know that I am God."* — Psalm 46:10 (KJV)
Calm your body. Anchor your spirit.

## Day 11 – Guard Your Peace

**Scripture:** *"Above all else, guard your heart."* — Proverbs 4:23 (NIV)
Limit noise. Protect emotional space.

## Day 12 – Practice Gratitude

**Scripture:** *"In every thing give thanks."* — 1 Thessalonians 5:18 (KJV)
Even in sorrow, gratitude stabilizes.

## Day 13 – Surrender Timing

**Scripture:** *"My times are in thy hand."* — Psalm 31:15 (KJV)
Trust what you cannot control.

## Day 14 – Anchor in Eternity

**Scripture:** *"Let not your heart be troubled."* — John 14:1–3 (KJV/NIV)
Separation in Christ is temporary.

# FOURTEEN DAYS AFTER THE FUNERAL

*(For the Quiet When the Crowds Have Left)*

## Day 1 – Rest Without Guilt

**Scripture:** *"Come unto me... and I will give you rest."* — Matthew 11:28 (KJV)
Shock lingers. Rest intentionally.

## Day 2 – Nourish Your Body

**Scripture:** *"I pray that you may enjoy good health."* — 3 John 1:2 (NIV)
Stabilize physically.

## Day 3 – Speak Their Name

**Scripture:** *"The righteous shall be in everlasting remembrance."* — Psalm 112:6 (KJV)
Memory is not betrayal.

## Day 4 – Walk in Light

**Scripture:** *"The Lord God is a sun and shield."* — Psalm 84:11 (KJV)
Ten minutes outside helps reset the nervous system.

## Day 5 – Journal Honestly

**Scripture:** *"Pour out your heart before him."* — Psalm 62:8 (KJV)
God can handle your raw words.

## Day 6 – Reach Out

**Scripture:** *"Two are better than one."* — Ecclesiastes 4:9 (KJV)
Isolation magnifies sorrow.

## Day 7 – Worship Through Tears

**Scripture:** *"Weeping may endure for a night, but joy cometh in the morning."* — Psalm 30:5 (KJV)
Tears and hope can coexist.

## Day 8 – Confront Distorted Thoughts

**Scripture:** *"Be transformed by the renewing of your mind."* — Romans 12:2 (KJV)
Answer lies with truth.

## Day 9 – Restore Structure

**Scripture:** *"Let all things be done decently and in order."* — 1 Corinthians 14:40 (KJV)
Routine protects stability.

## Day 10 – Guard Your Ears

**Scripture:** *"The wisdom from above is first pure, then peaceable."* — James 3:17 (KJV)
Reject harmful counsel.

### Day 11 – Steward Your Body Again

**Scripture:** *"Know ye not that your body is the temple of the Holy Ghost?"* — 1 Corinthians 6:19 (KJV)
Grief does not suspend stewardship.

### Day 12 – Reflect on Growth

**Scripture:** *"Count it all joy… when ye fall into divers temptations; knowing this, that the trying of your faith worketh patience."* — James 1:2–3 (KJV)
Suffering refines.

### Day 13 – Pray for Forward Strength

**Scripture:** *"I can do all things through Christ which strengtheneth me."* — Philippians 4:13 (KJV)
Ask for endurance, not escape.

### Day 14 – Declare Hope

**Scripture:** *"He will wipe every tear from their eyes. There will be no more death."* — Revelation 21:4 (NIV)
Death does not have the final word.

## Important Safety Note

If at any point you experience persistent hopelessness, inability to function, dangerous coping behaviors, or thoughts of self-harm, seek immediate professional help or emergency assistance in your area. Serious suffering requires serious listeners.

# RESOURCES

Grief does not follow a strict timeline, and healing often requires support beyond a single book. The following types of resources may provide additional guidance during your journey:

## Grief Counseling

Consider working with a **certified grief counselor** or **bereavement specialist** who focuses specifically on loss. Grief counseling can help you process complicated emotions, navigate anniversaries and triggers, and move forward without feeling like you are betraying the one you loved.

## Christian Counseling

If your grief includes spiritual confusion, anger toward God, or questions about eternity, a **board-certified Christian counselor** or trusted **biblically grounded therapist** may be especially helpful. Look for someone who honors Scripture while also understanding trauma, depression, and the realities of the grieving process.

## Trauma-Informed Therapy

Some losses are traumatic—especially sudden death, violent death, suicide, overdose, medical crisis, or witnessing suffering. A **trauma-informed therapist** can help with nightmares, panic, intrusive thoughts, and emotional shutdown. Trauma care is not the same as "just talking." It provides tools to calm the nervous system and rebuild stability.

## Pastoral Care

Engage with church leadership that combines spiritual maturity with emotional intelligence. Ask about experience in grief care, crisis response, and long-term support—not only funeral-day comfort.

## Support Groups

Grief support groups, whether church-based or community-based, offer shared understanding and reduce isolation. Being heard by others who understand loss can bring significant relief. Some people benefit most from **general grief groups**, while others prefer **specialized groups** (widows/widowers, loss of a child, miscarriage, suicide loss, caregiver grief, etc.).

## Medical Evaluation

If grief becomes overwhelming or symptoms of depression intensify, consult a qualified healthcare provider. Medication, when prescribed appropriately, may provide stabilization while deeper healing work continues. Sleep disruption, appetite changes, and prolonged fatigue also deserve medical attention.

## Crisis Support

If you or someone you know experiences thoughts of self-harm, inability to function, severe emotional distress, or dangerous substance use, seek **immediate assistance** from local emergency services or a crisis hotline in your area. Serious suffering requires serious listeners.

## Practical Guidance and Funeral Aftercare

Some families need support that is not only emotional but practical—help with paperwork, estates, survivor benefits, or funeral aftercare planning. Ask your funeral home, church, or local community resources about aftercare programs and referrals.

## Personal Practices

- Daily Scripture reading
- Intentional prayer
- Journaling
- Gentle physical movement
- Balanced nutrition and sleep
- Worship through music
- Trusted accountability relationships
- Time in sunlight and fresh air when possible
- Limiting isolation (even one safe connection weekly helps)

Grief is not a sign of weak faith. It is evidence of love. Seek help when needed. Walk steadily. Anchor yourself in truth.

# SELECTED REFERENCES

(Research and Clinical Foundations Referenced in This Work)

The reflections and insights in this book are grounded in established grief research, biblical theology, and professional experience within funeral service and Christian counseling. The five stages of grief referenced throughout the text originate from the work of Dr. Elisabeth Kübler-Ross, whose research on death and dying significantly shaped modern understanding of bereavement. While her stages are not linear or universally experienced in the same order, they provide a helpful framework for understanding emotional responses to loss.

Discussions of depression, antidepressant use, and psychoeducation reflect widely accepted principles in contemporary mental health practice. Readers are encouraged to consult licensed healthcare providers for individualized evaluation and treatment when needed.

All Scripture quotations are drawn from the King James Version (KJV) and the New International Version (NIV), as noted in the text.

Any references to contemporary worship music are included as thematic illustrations and not as formal lyrical citations.

The author's perspective is informed by years of professional work in funeral service, grief counseling, and direct engagement with families navigating death, loss, and the months that follow.

# SCRIPTURE INDEX

1. **John 14:1–3**
   "Let not your heart be troubled…"
   Chapter 2
2. **John 11:35**
   "Jesus wept."
   Chapter 2
3. **Isaiah 53:3**
   "A man of sorrows, and acquainted with grief…"
   Chapter 2
4. **Ephesians 4:26**
   "Be ye angry, and sin not…"
   Chapter 4
5. **Romans 8:1**
   "There is now no condemnation for those who are in Christ Jesus."
   Chapter 5
6. **Psalm 139:13–16**
   "All the days ordained for me were written in your book…"
   Chapter 5
7. **Matthew 5:4**
   "Blessed are those who mourn…"
   Chapter 9
8. **1 Corinthians 6:19–20**
   "Know ye not that your body is the temple of the Holy Ghost…?"
   Chapter 8
9. **Psalm 30:5**
   "Weeping may endure for a night, but joy cometh in the morning."
   Chapter 13

10. **1 Thessalonians 4:13–18**
    "Do not grieve like the rest of mankind, who have no hope."
    Chapter 2
11. **Revelation 21:3–4**
    "He will wipe every tear from their eyes."
    Chapter 14

# MUSIC REFERENCES

1. Marvin Sapp — *Never Would Have Made It*
   Chapter 2
2. Kirk Franklin — referenced regarding perseverance through imperfect faith
   Chapter 2
3. "Lord, Do It For Me" — referenced as prayerful surrender in weakness
   Chapter 6
4. Tasha Cobbs Leonard (ft. Jimi Cravity) — *You Know My Name*
   Chapter 9
5. Vicki Yohe — *Because of Who You Are*
   Chapter 10
6. VaShawn Mitchell — *Nobody Greater*
   Chapter 10

# SELECTED REFERENCES

American Psychiatric Association. *Diagnostic and Statistical Manual of Mental Disorders, Fifth Edition, Text Revision (DSM-5-TR).* Washington, DC: American Psychiatric Association, 2022.

Kübler-Ross, Elisabeth. *On Death and Dying.* New York: Scribner, 1969.

Kübler-Ross, Elisabeth, and David Kessler. *On Grief and Grieving: Finding the Meaning of Grief Through the Five Stages of Loss.* New York: Scribner, 2005.

Shear, M. Katherine. *Complicated Grief Treatment: The Theory, Practice, and Outcomes.* New York: Guilford Press, 2010.

Stroebe, Margaret, and Henk Schut. "The Dual Process Model of Coping with Bereavement." *Death Studies* 23, no. 3 (1999): 197–224.

Worden, J. William. *Grief Counseling and Grief Therapy: A Handbook for the Mental Health Practitioner.* 5th ed. New York: Springer Publishing Company, 2018.

Mayo Clinic Staff. "Complicated Grief." Mayo Clinic, updated medical guidance on prolonged grief and physiological stress responses.

Cleveland Clinic. "Grief and the Body: Physical Symptoms of Bereavement." Clinical health guidance resource.

www.ingramcontent.com/pod-product-compliance
Lightning Source LLC
LaVergne TN
LVHW010941110826
845149LV00013B/2701
*9798994630938*